THE COMMON

Phoenix Poets

A SERIES EDITED BY ROBERT VON HALLBERG

GAIL MAZUR

the
Common

The University of Chicago Press
Chicago & London

Gail Mazur lives and teaches in Cambridge, Massachusetts, where she is founder and director of The Blacksmith House Poetry Center. She is the author of two books of poetry: *Nightfire* (1978) and *The Pose of Happiness* (1986).

The University of Chicago Press, Chicago 60637
The University of Chicago Press, Ltd., London
© 1995 by The University of Chicago
All rights reserved. Published 1995
Printed in the United States of America

04 03 02 01 00 99 98 97 96 95   1 2 3 4 5

ISBN 0–226–51438–2 (cloth)
    0–226–51439–0 (paper)

Library of Congress Cataloging-in-Publication Data

Mazur, Gail.
    The common / Gail Mazur.
    p. cm. — (Phoenix poets)
    I. Title. II. Series
    PS3563.A987C65 1995
    811'.54—dc20   94-33930
                                 CIP

for Michael, and for Rebecca

Contents

three

four

Acknowledgments

Various poems in this volume originally appeared in the following periodicals and anthologies.

Agni Review: "At Boston Garden, the First Night of War, 1991,"
        "Family Plot," "I'm a Stranger Here Myself,"
        "Phonic"; © AGNI
American Voice: "Desire," "Why You Travel"
Atlantic Monthly: "Bluebonnets"
Boston Phoenix: "The Common"
Boston Review: "Poem for Christian, My Student," "Revenant,"
        "Two Worlds: A Bridge"
Boulevard: "In Houston"
Cimarron Review: "Yahrzeit," reprinted here with the permission
        of the Board of Regents for Oklahoma State University,
        holders of the copyright.
Colorado Review: "Fracture Santa Monica"
Cream City Review: "Pennies from Heaven"
Greensboro Review: "A Green Watering Can"
Harvard Review: "The Acorn"
Mississippi Review: "Bedroom at Arles"
Paris Review: "Blue," "Snake in the Grass"
Partisan Review: "Lilacs on Brattle Street" (vol. LX, no. 1, 1993)

Ploughshares: "After the Storm, August," "Poem Ending with
   Three Lines of Wordsworth's" (both in vol. 14, no. 4),
   "Traces" (vol. 14, no. 1), "Whatever They Want"
   (vol. 17, nos. 2 and 3)
Poetry: "Another Tree," "Foliage," "Ice," "A Small Plane from
   Boston to Montpelier," "Ware's Cove"
Poughkeepsie Review: "Maternal," "Mensch in the Morning"
Provincetown Arts: "May, Home after a Year Away"

Anthologies

  "Family Plot," "May, Home after a Year Away," and
"Phonic" appear in *New American Poets of the Nineties,* edited by
Jack Myers and Roger Weingarten (Boston, MA: David R. Godine,
Publishers, 1991).
  "Poem Ending with Three Lines of Wordsworth's" is
included in *The Roth American Poetry Annual, 1990* (Boston and
London: Faber & Faber).
  "The Idea of Florida During a Winter Thaw" appears in
*Hummers, Knucklers and Slow Curves: An Anthology of Contem-
porary Baseball Poetry,* edited by Don Johnson (Champaign:
University of Illinois Press, 1991). It also appears in *Diamonds Are a
Girl's Best Friend: Women Writers on Baseball,* edited by Elinor
Nauen (London: Faber & Faber, 1994).
  "Lilacs on Brattle Street" appears in *The Pushcart Prize,
XVIII, 1994,* edited by Bill Henderson (Wainscott, NY: Pushcart
Press).

THE COMMON

Two Worlds: A Bridge

Puffed-up windbags, black feathered bellows,
wheezy hinges: fierce yellow-eyed unlovable
inexpressibly expressive grackles.

Texas.
Oil-tainted air.
                            Premonitory luxury
of leaving a life. Floating alone
at night in my air-conditioned space
capsule, unknown
for a thousand miles.

Addison Street. Dryden. Wordsworth.
Shakespeare. Auden. Swamp
mysteriously re-constituted—
a British literary map.

Banana trees. Cottonwood.
Mesquite. Blue Gum.
Tallow. Chinaberry.

Mornings at a formica table,
reading obituaries for pleasure
of the *Chronicle's* names: Pamula.
Euphie. Bubba Levine.
Billy Jo Tardy.

Was that me in the Buffalo Cafe,
laughing at death?

And walking after the day's heat,
a thousand furious grackles flaring up,
clacking, frantic at my approach,
landing—
             black iridescent blooms
in the branching candelabra
of Rice Boulevard's great live oaks.

Half a country's distance
between the body and its biography.

At first, the body's baby-ish tissue,
its nervous Boston muscles,
begged to be taken home.

But that was only the body.

one

The Acorn

On the way home from school, a child is struck
on the head by a falling acorn. She looks down
at her brown shoes, refusing to give the squirrel—
who must have waited for her, aimed at her—
satisfaction. *You've got to show them you don't care*
her mother taught her. Does this mean
the squirrel knows she's Jewish? She always
dawdles so the other girls who have friends
to walk home with won't bully or taunt her
the way the Leblanc boys did yesterday,
in front of Corpus Christi—
pulling her hair, kicking her, calling her
"kike" and "Christ killer," while Father John
strolled up and down the sidewalk
that glittered with flecks of mica, reading.
Or the way Anna and Mary, the twins, held her down
in the cloakroom to make her show them her tail,
only letting go when the art teacher saw them.
Some days, she wants to be Catholic and make
confessions. Some of the secrets she keeps
from her mother. Why hurt her and what could she do?
Don't be fooled by girls pretending they like you,
the world is full of those rotten bitches—
The acorn.

I'm a Stranger Here Myself

Sometimes when you stop for directions,
when you ask someone who doesn't look
threatening or threatened the way to a gas
station or restaurant, the person stares at you,
dumbly, or seems apologetic or guilty,
and says these words as if they'd been
scripted: *I'm a stranger here myself*—, shaking
her head, or his head, and you're especially struck
by the bond between you, your strangeness,
and the town, or city, changes to unnumbered
anonymous facades, but generic, unmistakably
New England—white clapboard houses, black shutters;
or Texas storefronts—low porches, two-by-four columns,
longhorn arches; or even Southern California,
the faces its bungalows make, the expressive mouths
of, say, Los Angeles doors—and suddenly you want
to live there, wherever *there* is, to belong
in one place, to read the surviving daily,
you want to get a grip on the local mores,
to pay taxes, to vote, you want to have cronies,
be tired together in the Stormy Harbor
Coffee Shop, to be bored with the daily specials:
you want not to be like *him,* or *her,* not the outsider
who's never sure where things are; so you say,
"Thanks, anyway," and find the worn face of a
native who'll point you to a real estate office,

which hadn't been where you were going—
But then, you stop cold, scared, wanting
only your own room, the books under the bed,
the pencils, the snapshots, what's left
of your family, the dead flies on the windowsills,
the exhausted scorched-coffee smell of your city,
familiar as your own particular dust—and you turn
on a dime, shaking off Church Street and School Street,
the allegorical buildings, the knick-knack bookshelves
in the glowing blue family rooms blind to the moonlit
Main Street night, the lonely, confused, censorious
American-ness of places you drive through, where
you can get ice cream or a flat fixed, places where
strangers get hurt, so you jump back into your car
and head out to the highway, until the town,
that stage-set that almost swallowed you,
disappears at last in the fogged rearview mirror,
and you drive to the next and the next and the next,
fleeing that vicarious life for your life.

Mensch in the Morning

He seems glad of the splay of sun and my attention;
playful but purposeful.

Chasing his tail,
he also pretends to ignore it,

then spins in the wooden cage of my chair's legs,
trapping the thing

with a fast forepaw.
Again, he snubs it, faking absorption

in some abstraction—
motes in a light shaft.

Until he lets go,
he's stuck, of course,

all his rage focussed on his caboose.
Lucky kitten,

to keep forgetting the limitations
of his choices—

is that a sign of health?
Now he sets the tail loose—

a part of him suddenly sprung free!—
then whips around to ambush himself.

In Houston

I'd dislocated my life, so I went to the zoo.
It was December but it wasn't December. Pansies
just planted were blooming in well-groomed beds.
Lovers embraced under the sky's Sunday blue.
Children rode around and around on pastel trains.
I read the labels stuck on every cage the way
people at museums do, art being less interesting
than information. Each fenced-in plot had a map,
laminated with a stain to tell where in the world
the animals had been taken from. Rhinos waited
for rain in the rhino-colored dirt, too grief-struck
to move their wrinkles, their horns too weak
to ever be hacked off by poachers for aphrodisiacs.
Five white ducks agitated the chalky waters
of a duck pond with invisible orange feet
while a little girl in pink ruffles
tossed pork rinds at their disconsolate backs.

This wasn't my life! I'd meant to look
with the wise tough eye of exile, I wanted
not to anthropomorphize, not to equate, for instance,
the lemur's displacement with my displacement.
The arched aviary flashed with extravagance,
plumage so exuberant, so implausible, it seemed
cartoonish, and the birdsongs unintelligible,
babble, all their various languages unravelling—
no bird can get its song sung right, separated from
models of its own species.

For weeks I hadn't written a sentence,
for two days I hadn't spoken to an animate thing.
I couldn't relate to a giraffe—
I couldn't look one in the face.
I'd have said, if anyone had asked,
I'd been mugged by the Gulf climate.
In a great barren space, I watched a pair
of elephants swaying together, a rhythm
too familiar to be mistaken, too exclusive.
My eyes sweated to see the bull, his masterful trunk
swinging, enter their barn of concrete blocks,
to watch his obedient wife follow. I missed
the bitter tinny Boston smell of first snow,
the huddling in a cold bus tunnel.

At the House of Nocturnal Mammals,
I stepped into a furtive world of bats,
averted my eyes at the gloomy dioramas,
passed glassed-in booths of lurking rodents—
had I known I'd find what I came for at last?
How did we get here, dear sloth, my soul, my sister?
Clinging to a tree-limb with your three-toed feet,
your eyes closed tight, you calm my idleness,
my immigrant isolation. But a tiny tamarin monkey
who shares your ersatz rainforest runs at you,
teasing, until you move one slow, dripping,
hairy arm, then the other, the other, the other,
pulling your tear-soaked body, its too-few
vertebrae, its inferior allotment of muscles
along the dead branch, going almost nowhere
slowly as is humanly possible, nudged
by the bright orange primate taunting, nipping,
itching at you all the time, like ambition.

Whatever They Want

Tonight, my students can ask me anything.
I'll tell them the story of my life,
whatever they want. Outside, traffic shimmers
in the Gulf haze, mosquitoes incubate
in the bayou. My students laugh softly
at the broad *a* of my accent, evidence—
if they need it—of my vulnerability,
a woman fallible enough to be
their mother. And it's easy, I'm easy
with their drawled interrogations,
their curiosity, the way they listen
without memory or desire every Monday,
while I peel another layer from the onion,
the tearjerker, while the air conditioner
in the classroom stirs the fine hairs
on their arms, and I forget the cool protections
of irony, giving them my suffering family,
my appendectomy, my transcendent first kisses—
What kind of teaching is this?
I transport them with me to Maine,
to the Ukraine, they see my great uncle's
dementia, my cat's diabetes—exotica
of gloom, pratfalls, romantic fantasias,
extravagant sleet, snow, sweet innuendoes. . . .
They ask for it, they want to tell me things, too,
Texas stories, with boots, with dead fathers

and shrimp boats, with malls, with grackles,
with fire ants, with ice houses, with neon,
with rifles, and the Holy Scriptures—
Inexhaustible reality!
When I drive home singing past the palm trees
and the tenebrous live oaks and the tacquerias,
I'm in the movies, and later, when I sleep,
I dream of my babies, their insatiable hungers,
I give them permission to say whatever they want,
as long as there's no meanness in it,
as long as words taste bittersweet,
as long as they're true, as long as they move me.

Desire

It was a kind of torture—waiting
to be kissed. A dark car parked away
from the street lamp, away from our house
where my tall father would wait, his face
visible at a pane high in the front door.
Was my mother always asleep? A boy
reached for me, I leaned eagerly into him,
soon the windshield was steaming.

Midnight. A neighbor's bedroom light
goes on, then off. The street is quiet. . . .

Until I married, I didn't have my own key,
that wasn't how it worked, not at our house.
You had to wake someone with the bell,
or he was there, waiting. Someone let you in.
Those pleasures on the front seat of a boy's
father's car were "guilty," yet my body knew
they were the only right thing to do,

my body hated the cage it had become.

One of those boys died in a car crash;
one is a mechanic; one's a musician.
They were young and soft and, mostly, dumb.
I loved their lips, their eyebrows, the bones
of their cheeks, cheeks that scraped mine raw,
so I'd turn away from the parent who let me
angrily in. And always, the next day,

no one at home could penetrate the fog
around me. I'd relive the precious night
as if it were a bridge to my new state
from the old world I'd been imprisoned by,
and I've been allowed to walk on it, to cross
a border—there's an invisible line
in the middle of the bridge, in the fog,
where I'm released, where I think I'm free.

Bedroom at Arles

A painting he thought would rest the brain,
or rather, the imagination—

sloped room, chrome-yellow bed,
poppy-red coverlet, his own pictures

hung askew, or painted as if they were.
He'd splash cold water from the blue basin,

then take his blue smock from the peg.
Whole days outdoors he spoke to no one,

straining, as he had to, alone,
for *the high yellow note....*

Decades ago, I longed to be like him—
an isolate, a genius; beneath a poster

of his raw crooked room, I planned
a life, a monk's life, a vocation.

I was sure craziness was a side issue,
like the mistral's dust that whitened trees,

that drove him indoors to paint—
an obstacle yet, oddly, fine.

Now it seems a century's gone by
since I read his daily diary

of pictures,
that fevered year at Arles—

blue cypresses, apricot orchards,
Arlesienne faces. This bedroom.

A century, at least,
since I underestimated danger

and quarantined myself in the one room,
trying on a little madness, a little despair,

waking in the fictive mornings,
not awake yet to light like his—yellows

like sulphur, like lemons, like fresh butter,
not golden, or blazing, but homely—

Poem for Christian, My Student

He reminds me of someone I used to know,
but who? Before class,
he comes to my office to shmooze,
a thousand thousand pointless interesting
speculations. Irrepressible boy,
his assignments are rarely completed,
or actually started. This week, instead
of research in the stacks, he's performing
with a reggae band that didn't exist last week.
Kids danced to his music
and stripped, he tells me gleefully,
high spirit of the street festival.
He's the singer, of course—
why ask if he studied an instrument?
On the brink of graduating with
an engineering degree (not, it turned out,
his forte), he switched to English,
his second language. It's hard to swallow
the bravura of his academic escapes
or tell if the dark eyes laugh with his face.
Once, he brought me a tiny persimmon
he'd picked on campus; once, a poem
about an elderly friend in New Delhi
who left him volumes of Tagore
and memories of avuncular conversation.
My encouragement makes him skittish—

it doesn't suit his jubilant histrionics
of despair. And I remember myself
shrinking from enthusiasm or praise,
the prospect of effort—drudgery.
Success—a threat. A future, we figure,
of revision—yet what can the future be
but revision and repair? Now, on the brink
again, graduation's postponed, the brilliant
thesis on Walker Percy unwritten.
"I'll drive to New Orleans and soak
it up and write my paper in a weekend,"
he announces in the Honors office.
And, "I want to be a bum in daytime
and a reggae star at night!"
What could I give him from my life
or art that matters, how share
the desperate slumber of my early years,
the flashes of inspiration and passion
in a life on hold? If I didn't fool
myself or anyone, no one could touch
me, or tell me much . . . This gloomy
Houston Monday, he appears at my door,
so sunny I wouldn't dare to wake him
now, or say it matters if he wakes at all.
"Write a poem about me!" he commands,
and so I do.

May, Home after a Year Away

Bridal wreath. White rhododendron. Dogwood.
My town. At dawn, six or seven people—
hard to know if one shape's just a bundle—
sleeping on the Common's tender new grass
and on the granite benches. Dandelion
puffs cluster in the green—didn't we once
take deep breaths and blow the gossamer off
and make a wish? With each return home,
I seem to love it more, with less terror.

What would I wish for now? What wasn't working
still isn't. My friends' sorrows, mine again.
If only we could carry this sweet spring
in us anywhere . . . I hope I die in May, some
one to scatter my ashes—
                              Is that it, Gail,
the wish you make in your happiness?

two

Bluebonnets

I lay down by the side of the road
in a meadow of bluebonnets, I broke
the unwritten law of Texas. My brother

was visiting, he'd been tired, afraid of
his tiredness as we'd driven toward Bremen,
so we stopped for the blue relatives

of lupine, we left the car on huge feet
we'd inherited from our lost father,
our Polish grandfather. Those flowers

were too beautiful to only look at;
we walked on them, stood in the middle
of them, threw ourselves down,

crushing them in their one opportunity
to thrive and bloom. We lay like angels
forgiven our misdeeds, transported

to azure fields, the only word for
the color eluded me—delft, indigo,
sapphire, some heavenly word you might

speak to a sky. I led my terrestrial brother
there to make him smile and this
is my only record of the event.

We took no pictures, we knew no camera
could fathom that blue. I brushed
the soft spikes, I fingered lightly

the delicate earthly petals, I thought,
This is what my hands do well
isn't it, touch things about to vanish.

Fracture Santa Monica

Don't walk like a drunken sailor,
my trainer scolds, as I lope across Ocean
Avenue, dreamscape of my lopsided autumn.

Odd men and women swathed in blankets applaud
when I place the broken left foot in front
of the okay right, then reverse without a hitch

and walk backwards, toward the pier,
the polluted Pacific. Why, they're applauding
my ligaments, my courage! The way I back into

traffic, the traffic signal's bird-cheeps
saving my life! They rise from their bedrolls
of stains and infirmity and the clapping

dies. *Heel, toe! heel, toe! heel, toe!*
I back through the detritus, the eucalyptus,
the *cirque du soleil* spinning behind me.

What's to be glad about or proud of
when the smallest dire injury begins
my downhill glide to self-pity, to hyperboles

of despair? I'm a parvenu, a cat-scratch
in this seascape of amputations, I'm
selfish, selfish, the trainer snaps,

What are you good for, dragging in the sand?
Who's it gonna help if you fix that foot?

The Idea of Florida During a Winter Thaw

Late February, and the air's so balmy
snowdrops and crocuses might be fooled
into early blooming. Then, the inevitable blizzard
will come, blighting our harbingers of spring,
and the numbed yards will go back undercover.
In Florida, it's strawberry season—
shortcake, waffles, berries and cream
will be penciled on the coffeeshop menus.

In Winter Haven, the ballplayers are stretching
and preening, dancing on the basepaths,
giddy as good kids playing hookey. Now,
for a few weeks, statistics won't seem
to matter, for the flushed boys are muscular
and chaste, lovely as lakes to the retired men
watching calisthenics from the grandstands.
Escapees from the cold work of living,

the old men burnish stories of Yaz and the Babe
and the Splendid Splinter. For a few dreamy dollars,
they sit with their wives all day in the sun,
on their own little seat cushions, wearing soft caps
with visors. Their brave recreational vehicles
grow hot in the parking lot, though they're
shaded by live oaks and bottlebrush trees
whose soft bristles graze the top-racks.

At four, the spectators leave in pairs, off
to restaurants for Early Bird Specials.
A salamander scuttles across the quiet
visitors' dugout. The osprey whose nest is atop
the foul pole relaxes. She's raged all afternoon
at balls hit again and again toward her offspring.
Although December's frost killed the winter crop,
there's a pulpy orange-y smell from juice factories. . . .

Down the road, at Cypress Gardens, a woman
trainer flips young alligators over on their backs,
demonstrating their talent for comedy—stroke
their bellies, they're out cold, instantaneously
snoozing. A schoolgirl on vacation gapes,
wonders if she'd ever be brave enough
to try that, to hold a terrifying beast
and turn it into something cartoon-funny.

She stretches a hand toward the toothy sleeper
then takes a step back, to be safe as she reaches.

Snake in the Grass

—I'd screamed when it slithered under my hand
as I leaned to pick the first ripe blueberry.
It was noon, a Monday in late July. The sun,
as always, was hot on my shoulders, hot
on the back of my blouse. I'd forgotten
the universe wasn't all dead pines and Indian
graves and boarded-up houses, that I wasn't
the only creature left alive in it, that I'd
never found my comfortable place inside it.
I wanted to be someone who doesn't scare,
who can't be shaken, so I wanted no witnesses
to this paradigm in the Garden. Then, the snake
slid noiselessly under the rotting porch
of our family cottage. The reduced summer woods,
the wide sky, were stunned and silent. Imagine
a silence, all you hear your own scream vanishing.
A second before, you'd knelt to the ground,
humming, and something writhed at your left hand,
wild as migraine, while your right reached
through transparent air to the first sweet berry,
treasure of asthmatic childhood's summers.
It isn't death you fear now, or years ago,
it's the sneak attack, the large hand clapped
over your mouth, bad moments that suddenly
come back when you think you're at home
in the frayed landscape you've already lost,

and a snake, a *not-you,* invisible, camouflaged
in the famished grass, jolts you out of your dream.
Try being rational and patient:
get into your car, drive down the old road
to Dunroamin' Campgrounds. You've got a quarter—
telephone a friend, he'll probably be in
his amber-lit air-conditioned office, reading
student papers. He might say postmodernism's
days are numbered, but he'd like to get away.
Tell him not to come down to the Cape.
Tell him about the harmless snake, give him
the scream, how you blushed that one of nature's
creatures should think you're a silly woman.
Embellish a little, laugh at yourself in the hot
glass booth. There'll be kids playing volleyball
on the parched field, mosquitoes, mothers
spreading mustard on baloney sandwiches.
—Wouldn't anyone have screamed at the chill
reptilian underhand move of that snake?
Wasn't that scream waiting for years?
Can't you relent, can't you love yet
your small bewildering part in this world?

Blue

Once I thought there was no blue in nature
except the sky—I thought Nature couldn't make
a blue flower, or tree, or creature.

I was young and hadn't looked at anything—

that was before I knew delphiniums
and morning glories, before I'd heard the bluejays,
or recognized the steadfast spruce trees,

or knew about Nabokov's butterflies.

Before my blue cat, I didn't know color
has its own vocabulary in every language:
his mother was a Russian Blue,

and often, when I'd been out a while,
the delirious syllables of his blueness
would amaze me at the door—

it's always so hard to remember color exactly. . . .

His coat couldn't be described by any synonyms
or tropes for gray, not mist or fog,
not colorless, not ash—

although I've buried his ashes in the pitch-
dark shade of our yard where hot summer days
he loved to lie, happy

to be cool yet close to me,

and I'm going to plant a juniper nearby,
not really to remind me, but that every autumn
the place where he lay might be

lit by the electric-blue of its leaf.

Why You Travel

You don't want the children to know how afraid
you are. You want to be sure their hold on life

is steady, sturdy. Were mothers and fathers
always this anxious, holding the ringing

receiver close to the ear: *Why don't they answer,
where could they be?* There's a conspiracy

to protect the young, so they'll be fearless,
it's why you travel—it's a way of trying

to let go, of lying. You don't sit
in a stiff chair and worry, you keep moving.

Postcards from the Alamo, the Alhambra.
Photos of you in Barcelona, Gaudi's park

swirling behind you. There you are in the Garden
of the Master of the Fishing Nets, one red

tree against a white wall, koi swarming
over each other in the thick demoralized pond.

You, fainting at the Buddhist caves.
Climbing with thousands on the Great Wall,

wearing a straw cap, a backpack, a year
before the students at Tiananmen Square.

Having the time of your life, blistered and smiling.
The acid of your fear could eat the world.

After the Storm, August

What can I learn from the hummingbird,
a big thing like me? I hardly have time
to study its flash, its momentous
iridescence, before it disappears
into the mimosa, sated with nectar.
I admire the way the greenery trembles.
I remember reading that this bird is
never sated—its whole miniature
life an exercise in digestion. What
excuse does it need to be this useless,
what's to learn from this inscrutable engine?
Why does something in me fly out
to the feathery tree, whirring
so hungrily toward translucence?

three

A Green Watering Can

It's evening.

The day visitors have come, wept,
and left their wilted flowers.
He's found a green watering can
(like mine, with a long curved spout)
tossed in a corner of the caretaker's shack.

He fills it from the empty tap—
someone has to tend these thirsty graves,
the old ones no one visits. . . .
He works haplessly, as in life,
but with sweetness and good humor,

with certainty that whatever he cares for
will thrive and grow. He smiles
his lovely weightless smile, looking
at the crooked mess of annuals
his wife left, and his daughter.

My father is telling the crickets
and the night slitherers,
Human beings never change,
but you can learn to love them.
This is the retirement he didn't live

to enjoy, where he'd impart wisdom
to his children and grandchildren
who cried pitifully when he died,
knowing now he couldn't teach them
how to become good men and women.

The dead are so efficient,
they step lightly here,
they know their way around the stones
the way the long-blind
can navigate their homes.

Here it's true nothing changes:
a hole is dug then it's filled;
a small crowd comes and always goes away.

Then my father brings out the mower
with its feathery blades. No one
likes a neat lawn better than he did,
sweating under the July sun.

I'd believe this story—
but that's not my green watering can
nourishing the hopeful dead.

Maternal

On the telephone, friends mistake us now
when we first say hello—not after.
And that oddly optimistic lilt
we share nourishes my hopes:
we do *sound* happy. . . .

Last night, in my dream's crib,
a one-day infant girl.
I wasn't totally unprepared—
there was the crib, and cotton kimonos,
not just a padded dresser drawer.

And then, I knew I could drive
to the store for the tiny, funny
clothes my daughter wears.

I was in a familiar room
and leaned over the rail, crooning
Hello, and the smiling baby—
she'd be too young for speech,
I know, or smiles—
gurgled back at me, *Hullo.*

—If I could begin again,
I'd hold her longer, closer!

Maybe that way, when night opens
into morning, and all my windows
gape at the heartbreaking street,
my dreams wouldn't pierce so,

I wouldn't hold my breath
at the parts of my life still in hiding,
my childhood's white house
where I lunged toward the flowers of love
as if I were courting death. . . .

Over the crib, a mobile was spinning,
bright birds going nowhere,
primary colors, primary
as mothering once seemed. . . .

Later, I wonder why I dreamt
that dream, yearning for what I've had,
and have

why it was my mother's room,
the blonde moderne bedroom set
hidden under years of junk—a spare room's
the nicest way to put it,

though now all
her crowded rooms are spare—

Ware's Cove

Odd, to find the little square snapshot caught
in the back of a dresser drawer:
my grandfather (I'd been thinking of him)

dwarfed in an Adirondack chair on the dock.
My father would have set him up there,
holding a bamboo fishing pole,

and had the old black Kodak ready.
It would have been a Sunday during the War.
Across the river, feverish woods

and the changing house aren't in the picture.
Nor kids, screaming and splashing
while a lifeguard dozes on his tower.

Once, when the cove was dammed,
the whole neighborhood came down
to rake the riverbed which was mined

with broken bottles. My brother's feet
and mine still bear the moon-shaped scars.
Later, a girl drowned there.

At night, I'd picture the disconnected
body, memorizing Red Cross rescues
that would never beat the river's current.

Now there's no one I love
to say what fish grandfather caught
in the not-yet polluted water,

and no one—not anyone living
in the identical, stupid houses
squeezed side to vinyl side

where the innocent woods once were—
no one can have swum here since.
There is no blue-lipped boy,

skinny and shivering, no hopeful girl,
no vigilant mother with Noxema
and towels and tears, calling her in.

Ice

In the warming house, children lace their skates,
bending, choked, over their thick jackets.

A Franklin stove keeps the place so cozy
it's hard to imagine why anyone would leave,

clumping across the frozen beach to the river.
December's always the same at Ware's Cove,

the first sheer ice, black, then white
and deep until the city sends trucks of men

with wooden barriers to put up the boys'
hockey rink. An hour of skating after school,

of trying wobbly figure-8's, an hour
of distances moved backwards without falling,

then—twilight, the warming house steamy
with girls pulling on boots, their chafed legs

aching. Outside, the hockey players keep
playing, slamming the round black puck

until it's dark, until supper. At night,
a shy girl comes to the cove with her father.

Although there isn't music, they glide
arm in arm onto the blurred surface together,

braced like dancers. She thinks she'll never
be so happy, for who else will find her graceful,

find her perfect, skate with her
in circles outside the emptied rink forever?

Traces

Sometimes I have delusions
of total recall, tyrannical, crazy.

Crazy is what I thought years ago,
"You're crazy!"
when I built a home
over my father's bulldozed house.

Nothing's ever lost to me,
certainly not the arsonned pieces of that place
that erupt like clocks
in the rockiness of my yard.

Yesterday, yellowed linoleum
bloomed in the herb garden—
his much-scrubbed kitchen tile;

and this morning, by the door,
I found a porcelain shard,
part of the upstairs bath.

Commonplace relics,
they hide themselves in a common grave,
then, break out on my path;

they bide their time, they just won't quit,
not while I live—
burnt scraps, artifacts, detritus—
they're memory's arsenal
stockpiled under sumac and ferns. . . .

A bit of blue China makes me shiver,

its graceful willow
drooping over two fishermen
pacing a broken blue bridge,

once the perfect world
I pushed and poked mashed turnips around—

Oh, unfathomable figures
so displaced below me,
so fixed in their pitiless purposes!

Phonic

As if my answering machine were a rejection,
you'd leave your forlorn message:
Call your father. . . . Then, a dial tone.
Guilty of being out, or busy,
I never thought to save the tape,
to keep some resonance and pitch of you,
if only in those four syllables—
tremulous, demanding, but tangible

as the snapshots I found today,
a torn dwarf, her plump gray face
shadowing as she squatted on our front porch,
tight braids, strange frown, white Mary Janes.

I'd forgotten that silent child
until I held her flattened image.
My peopled past is curled and tattered,
tucked into envelopes and albums;
it reconstitutes itself in dreams,
a *richesse* of repeat performances—
a friend's touch become sweetly erotic,
my children, peachy and clinging again,

you, saying you're not afraid of dying. . . .
I wish I could listen to your voice
instead of the staticky measures
of a cassette's repetitive erasures—

although sometimes in my edgy sleep,
I hear a *Gail!* that snaps me awake:
an urgent extrasensory appeal
I take for mortal emergency.
I feel sure it's you, calling
for something I don't understand
and never did. Then, it disappears.
The voice is nowhere in my wakefulness,

not kept in memory's burr—
no tender disinterested utterance
you never quite pulled off in life,
good as you were.

Pennies from Heaven

So when you hear it thunder
don't run under a tree—
there'll be pennies from heaven
for you and me!

Every time it rains,
I hear the buoyant promise of that song,
sung off-key before a shaving mirror,
or played on a scratchy RCA Victrola—
memory of someone else's memory,
the first year of his marriage, after
the Crash, after both fathers' businesses
went under. Pennies from heaven, pies
in the sky his wife always knew
not to count on. I'll hum the tune,
thinking of them in the kitchen dancing
to music from their celluloid radio,
dancing the Continental from chairs
to table to chairs like Rogers and Astaire,
style they caught on their monthly sprees
at the Bijou. Those nights they'd glide home
through the 'Thirties streets, and if it rained,
the dirty town looked lucky as new pennies.
Did they know their youth was a kind of money?
And if they knew, could they choose
how to save or use it? In a few years,
there were three babies, the War,

and the sunny, cheerful man driving
the New England territory, taking orders,
selling. They bought a house with shutters
on a river where weekend mornings
he'd croon like Crosby to his middle child,
a daughter, while he shaved, and I worshiped
from a duck-shaped potty, memorizing
the lyrics of his philosophy. Or,
tired weeknights, he'd revive if I
parroted verses he'd taught me, perfect
tin-eared imitations and together we'd warble
our hopelessly hopeful harmony. . . .
So when I hear it thunder, I don't run
under a tree—I still see our blue-green
bathroom, the closed door, the towels,
I won't let it go, that steamy scene
where I am married to my father's dreaming.

Another Tree

If a tree dies, plant another one.
            —Linnaeus

We sat in the yard where his house had burned.

Only I had seen the shadowed negative,
the x-ray of his brain. He squinted,

one eye too sensitive to the sun.

His right hand lay useless on his lap.
Optimism all that was left to him,

all of his grace.

For him, I'd rescued and rebuilt the place,
made a new house, planted another tree,

the little mimosa now two stories high.

In a few weeks, he'd be gone,
such was the rapaciousness of the cells,

so defenseless the nervous system.

This was the yard, this the driveway,
where one summer of Saturdays, he gathered

minyans to say *Kaddish* for his mother.

He admired every thing living, he loved
the mimosa, the pan-sized hibiscus,

the woodpecker whose staccato knocks

are the punctuation of this memory.
I held his good left hand, still the dreamer,

"Look, what a miracle this hand is—"

he said, *"seventy years I hardly used it,
and now, the things it's learning to do!"*

We looked together at what was left,
at what was growing.

Revenant

I dreamt you died again, this time in a fire.
You left a note for Mother that didn't burn,
saying how you wanted us brought up.
She wouldn't show it to me, or tell what it said.

—But I was *there* in the blazing house,
we were all there together,
although the others slept through it.

Why didn't you save yourself?
Why couldn't I save you?

You died horribly, like all those people
in runway plane crashes, seared in death,
struggling for air, piled in heaps at the exits.

Again, Mother tried to build a new life—
she bought a Japanese car, permed her hair.
Then she went into hiding.

I wandered from barber to barber
until my hair was cut short
                              as when I was twelve
and picked up the manicure scissors in the bathroom
and scalloped myself—I had to—
then hung a towel over the mirror.

Yahrzeit

Tonight, after everyone leaves, I turn
off the lights and stay in my blue chair
to watch the last embers in the fireplace,
just as I sat two years ago keeping
the flame of my father's yahrzeit candle
company when the condolence callers had gone.
Alone that night in the wing chair I spoke
aloud to the faltering flame that had become
my father and was dying. I said some words
to a framed photograph of him standing
by an airplane with his hat and briefcase,
grinning and waving like a sweet ambassador,
going I don't know where. That October of death,
my family knew only to eat and mumble and rage
to erase his body's inexorable implosions.
I'd lit the plump candle stuck in a tumbler
marked with the star of David like the plain
wooden casket my brother and I had chosen.
It flamed for days until it began to sputter
and I whispered to it as I had to him,
Let go now, you can let go, and in the frozen
living room the frail light finally gave out. . . .
But today everything—the rackety bluejay
scavenging the yard, the dun and scarlet leaves
skirmishing in the street, the pale begonias
I'd thought to rescue from the fall's first frost—

everything felt so alive, flash and color
I've been blind to these two bereft Octobers.
I wanted to grab and hold what's left to me,
to hold it all as the sun brilliantly went down,
the new moon rose. And now, while the house cools,
I lean in to urge back to life the past's
wavering warmth, to poke at the delicate ash
though I know the fire has nothing to give,
and my grief flares, and lets go, like desire.

Family Plot

I'm digging at my father's grave,
my mother's holding the rusty mums
she's carried here to make a little garden

before the first frost. Three years today,
and the grass is a damp brown rectangle
over his cryptic body that's guarded

by earth from my more morbid speculations.
Perpetual care's contracted out here,
so no one's responsible for the dried-out

tap, the graveyard's shameless posture
of neglect, certainly not this pair
of purposeful mourners with trowels

and perennials we've chosen
for their profusions of unopened buds.
I'm not good at this, thudding my shovel

at stones, setting pots in the ground
off-center. Alone, I'd plant a little dogwood,
a Japanese drift of flowering branch

above his name, but my mother sees this
as her future home and wants, as usual,
something else, something harder to nurture.

I'll never lie here. I don't want anyone
to stand, icy-handed, imagining
my ruined body. My father liked so much

to laugh—would he enjoy his clumsy girl
hacking away at clumps of sod, or his wife's
sensible blue shoes sinking in mud?

It doesn't matter. I can't even say
if he or I believed in God,
or in any kind of hereafter. . . .

A drizzle mists the raw new hole,
mists the one white rose from my table,
and the pebble I place on his headstone

like a good Orthodox daughter
leaving a memorial relic
as if it were a talisman of devotion that

nothing—no eternities of neglect by
myself or others, no drought or blight
or storm or holocaust—could erode.

four

Foliage

Even the man who dozes on cardboard
in the Common, wearing a bright knit cap,
has picked Clover and Ladies' Thumb to stick
in the cosmos of his shopping cart.
These last warm days, wanting to deny
what's frozen and gray ahead, I admire
the star turns of my town's great trees.
Sunbursts, and the alizarin crimson

of our maples' explosions, a kind of payoff
(I want to think) for all the dying,
yet something I'm part of—part of me—
like my feet, planted deferentially
in this old park, my hands red at my sides,
my head nodding and shaking in the leafy air.

The Common

Iron cannons from the Revolution. Ghost music—
folk songs, rock concerts, Sunday demonstrations.
A granite slab for the elm where Washington

took command. A new wood plaque, already rotting,
for Margaret Fuller Ossoli—the city fathers'
minimal nod to the life of her mind.

The black trunks of old maples brushed with snow,
their strong lines rephrased by snow's finery.
From a concrete gazebo, Abraham Lincoln

gazes down at the cobbled plaza where raffish
bands plugged in, and stoned crowds gathered;
my small son and daughter skipped ahead

of me, hand in hand, to the swings, the jungle
gym, the roundabout, and at home, pre-season
jonquils dazzled in a white crockery jug.

Stringed beads—necklaces, earrings—for sale
by a woman who's sat cross-legged on folded blankets
since those days, those days.

The season's worst cold brewing this early morning.
Two men huddled in damp sleeping bags spread out
on newspapers; convulsive dreams of their war.

The oaks. The maples. In the near-zero day
I take on faith, faith in Nature, that life's
machinery groans and strains in the frozen limbs.

At Boston Garden, the First Night of War, 1991

Dank rank North Station.
Sausage and peppers, pizza, beer
in big waxed paper cups. Wet floors, wet wool coats.

Oily franks gleaming like trophies
on an overlit rotating grill. The last
rush-hour trains shaking the floor. Five minutes

since the first news, from TV's
hanging, hospital-style, from the ceiling.
Inside the Garden, on the fringe,

we sidle close to the athletes, measure
ourselves against the startling height, the players
warming up, hookshots, dunks, none

of the boyish joking and jostling.
Amplified organ music: *Yankee Doodle Dandy.*
Over There. This is the Army. Out here

in America, a crowd gathers for gratification,
for pleasures, then stirs and is stirred by songs.
Loudspeaker introductions and

"A moment to honor our fighting men and women."
Star Spangled Banner, trumpet flourishes:
And the rockets' red glare, the bombs bursting in air—

applause, tentative at first, then explosive.
(The body's sly, shy intelligence so easily confused.)
The words, lightbulbs blinking on a scoreboard.

Poem Ending with Three Lines of Wordsworth's

The organ donor who smiles
in the leathery dark of my wallet
from a driver's license

has already struck one woman—
elderly, confused—
who stumbled off a Somerville curb

one January dusk
and became a sickening thump,
then a bleeding body

cradled in the driver's arms
until police and ambulance came.
That old woman lived

to sue the driver who now
takes a different route each week
to the supermarket,

and on her birthday,
in line at the Registry, decides
she's old enough, if not

for a Living Will, then to leave
her kidneys or heart or liver;
the little silver label below her

Polaroid portrait is the Registry's
donor code. She envisions herself
extricated one night

from crushed burning metal
by the jaws of life
less lucky, finally, than her victim

whose two pocketbooks (maybe
she was a pursesnatcher?) flew
in opposite directions

and landed awfully far
from the eyeglasses and left shoe.
All the eyewitnesses

exonerated the driver.
They swore to what she won't remember:
the old woman fell,

or fainted to the fender;
the car was going five miles an hour.
Still, that impact was what she'd dreaded

all her tremulous years at the wheel
which she grips for dear guilty life,
concocting terms of a bargain—

she'll bequeath what she's got in her body
so whatever virtues she lacks,
she won't just be someone dead

unprofitably traveling toward the grave
like a false steward who has much received
and renders nothing back.

Lilacs on Brattle Street

On the brick sidewalk, pale clusters
of purple stars, picked carelessly
from nineteenth-century yards
by rootless flirtatious students,
tossed away, darkening, after a brief fling
with nature and the city's literary past. . . .

Brattle Street. "Tory Row." This afternoon,
I could almost think nothing's changed—
clouds of May cherry blossoms, pink dogwood,
the mellow blown tulips—so peaceful,
Longfellow himself might be strolling here,
lost in Dante, *nel mezzo del cammin* . . .
or Margaret Fuller, her father's only son,
breaking from studies in Greek and Latin,
not yet awakened to love, not yet drowned. . . .

A small boy tears past me, his arms full
of lavender plunder, lilacs he's bringing home
for his mother. I like his face
on which little but joy is written,
yet I have to invent a darkness in it,
as if, moments ago, he was dragging
his sneakered feet, desperate to forget
what his teacher said, something about Chernobyl.
She pointed to it on the roll-down Hammond map.
He was swept for the first time by the question
What if nothing lasts?

I make this innocent boy, this thief,
think my thoughts about nuclear ash
blowing across Kiev, across our ancestors.
I see him in the stunned classroom, terror
that passes when the bell rings, but we know
it will return now, over and over,
the too-bright light, eye-widening
what if—

what if everything in his world that matters
were colorless, empty, gone
like the wooden synagogues of Poland,
everything—the Victorian schoolhouse,
its airy unfair cage of gerbils; the 5&10
where he buys his models; his sister,
his sister waiting for him now on the front steps;
the houseplant his mother named for him yesterday
while she watered it—*Begonia*—its pink flowers
in the front window beside the gray cat
watching for him, too, planted there,
we think, since morning, since he left for school—
reliable, wily;
                        and his room upstairs,
his Marvel comics, his painted bookcase,
the plastic dinosaurs lined up on its shelves
like disguised lead soldiers—the fierce
triceratops, the mastodon, the inchling
woolly mammoth—replicas he loves from the set
his grandfather *May his soul rest in peace*
sent him last year . . .

A Small Plane from Boston to Montpelier

This twelve-seater wanders west of my childhood,
my used-up river snaking away
beyond the tinfoil wing;

ahead, the raking late afternoon,
the spiritual mass
of New Hampshire's mountains.

Isn't this how Bierstadt saw, and the others,
from horseback, or on foot,
when they set their easels up a century ago—

the light,
like a signal they believed in,
illuminating the stirring, snow-brushed peaks,

man in the landscape
tiny as a thistle.

What they'd fled—
the machine of the nineteenth century—
bucolic to us now,

and their God—
didn't he illuminate then
the implications of the cycles,

or,
promise something paradisical? . . .

This silvery pod,
hurtling past the clouds,
barely keeps us from the cold,

its wall a membrane icy to the touch,

and below,
a tiny plane like this one
zooms diagonally to its destination.